The Seven Against Thebes by Æschylus

Æschylus is often regarded as the father of Greek tragedy; he moved play writing from the simple interaction of a single character and a chorus to one where many characters interact and thereby create more dynamic and dramatic situations.

Æschylus, was the son of Euphorion, and a scion of a Eupatrid or noble family. He was born at Eleusis 525 B.C., or, as the Greeks calculated time, in the fourth year of the 63rd Olympiad.

He first worked at a vineyard and whilst there claimed to have been visited by Dionysis in a dream and told to turn his attention to the tragic art.

It was a dream that would deliver a rich and incredible legacy through his writing talents. His earliest tragedy, composed when he was twenty-six years of age, failed to win the fabled Dionysia, (a revered festival of theatre) and it was not until fifteen years later that he gained this victory in 484BC going on to win it again in 472 BC (for The Persians), 467 BC (for Seven Against Thebes) and 463 BC (for The Suppliants)

Æschylus was also known for his military skills and was ready to fight in defence of Athens whenever the call was made. He and his brother, Cynegeirus, fought against Darius's invading Persian army at the Battle of Marathon in 490 BCE and, although the Greeks won against overwhelming odds, Cynegeirus died in the battle, which had a naturally had a profound effect on Æschylus.

He made several visits to the important Greek city of Syracuse in Sicily at the invitation of the tyrant Hieron, and it is thought that he also travelled extensively in the region of Thrace.

His writing continued to be the envy of others. With the series of plays of which Seven Against Thebes was a part, his supremacy was undisputed. He was the "father of tragedy."

Æschylus made many changes to dramatic form. The importance of the chorus was demoted and a second added to give prominence to the dialogue and making that interchange the leading feature of the play. He removed all deeds of bloodshed from the public view, and in their place provided various spectacular elements, improving the costumes, making the masks more expressive and convenient, and probably adopting the cothurnus to increase the stature of the performers. Finally, he established the custom of contending for the prize with trilogies, an inter-connecting set of three independent dramas.

The closing years of the life of Æschylus were mainly spent in Sicily, which he had first visited soon after his defeat at the Dionysia by Sophocles.

Æschylus returned to Athens to produce his Orestean trilogy, probably the finest of his works, although the Eumenides, the last of the three plays, revealed so openly his aristocratic tendencies that he became extremely unpopular, and returned to Sicily for the last time in 458 BCE and it was there that he died, while visiting the city of Gela in 456 or 455 BCE.

Index of Contents

Æschylus – A Concise bibliography

THE PERSONS
ETEOCLES
A SPY
CHORUS OF CADMEAN MAIDENS
ANTIGONE
ISMENE
A HERALD

THE SEVEN AGAINST THEBES

ETEOCLES
Clansmen of Cadmus, at the signal given
By time and season must the ruler speak
Who sets the course and steers the ship of State
With hand upon the tiller, and with eye
Watchful against the treachery of sleep.
For if all go aright, thank Heaven, men say,
But if adversely—which may God forefend!—
One name on many lips, from street to street,
Would bear the bruit and rumour of the time,
Down with Eteocles!—a clamorous curse,
A dirge of ruin. May averting Zeus
Make good his title here, in Cadmus' hold!
You it beseems now boys unripened yet
To lusty manhood, men gone past the prime
And increase of the full begetting seed,
And those whom youth and manhood well combined
Array for action—all to rise in aid
Of city, shrines, and altars of all powers
Who guard our land; that ne'er, to end of time,
Be blotted out the sacred service due
To our sweet mother-land and to her brood.
For she it was who to their guest-right called
Your waxing youth, was patient of the toil,
And cherished you on the land's gracious lap,
Alike to plant the hearth and bear the shield
In loyal service, for an hour like this.
Mark now! until to-day, luck rules our scale;
For we, though long beleaguered, in the main
Have with our sallies struck the foemen hard.
But now the seer, the feeder of the birds,
(Whose art unerring and prophetic skill
Of ear and mind divines their utterance
Without the lore of fire interpreted)
Foretelleth, by the mastery of his art,

That now an onset of Achaea's host
Is by a council of the night designed
To fall in double strength upon our walls.
Up and away, then, to the battlements,
The gates, the bulwarks! don your panoplies,
Array you at the breast-work, take your stand
On floorings of the towers, and with good heart
Stand firm for sudden sallies at the gates,
Nor hold too heinous a respect for hordes
Sent on you from afar: some god will guard!
I too, for shrewd espial of their camp,
Have sent forth scouts, and confidence is mine
They will not fail nor tremble at their task,
And, with their news, I fear no foeman's guile.

[Enter **A SPY**.

THE SPY
Eteocles, high king of Cadmus' folk,
I stand here with news certified and sure
From Argos' camp, things by myself descried.
Seven warriors yonder, doughty chiefs of might,
Into the crimsoned concave of a shield
Have shed a bull's blood, and, with hands immersed
Into the gore of sacrifice, have sworn
By Ares, lord of fight, and by thy name,
Blood-lapping Terror, Let our oath be heard—
Either to raze the walls, make void the hold
Of Cadmus—strive his children as they may—
Or, dying here, to make the foemen's land
With blood impasted. Then, as memory's gift
Unto their parents at the far-off home,
Chaplets they hung upon Adrastus' car,
With eyes tear-dropping, but no word of moan.
For their steeled spirit glowed with high resolve,
As lions pant, with battle in their eyes.
For them, no weak alarm delays the clear
Issues of death or life! I parted thence
Even as they cast the lots, how each should lead,
Against which gate, his serried company.
Rank then thy bravest, with what speed thou may'st,
Hard by the gates, to dash on them, for now,
Full-armed, the onward ranks of Argos come!
The dust whirls up, and from their panting steeds
White foamy flakes like snow bedew the plain.
Thou therefore, chieftain! like a steersman skilled,
Enshield the city's bulwarks, ere the blast
Of war comes darting on them! hark, the roar
Of the great landstorm with its waves of men!
Take Fortune by the forelock! for the rest,
By yonder dawn-light will I scan the field

Clear and aright, and surety of my word
Shall keep thee scatheless of the coming storm.

ETEOCLES

O Zeus and Earth and city-guarding gods,
And thou, my father's Curse, of baneful might,
Spare ye at least this town, nor root it up,
By violence of the foemen, stock and stem!
For here, from home and hearth, rings Hellas' tongue.
Forbid that e'er the yoke of slavery
Should bow this land of freedom, Cadmus' hold!
Be ye her help! your cause I plead with mine—
A city saved doth honour to her gods!

[Exit **ETEOCLES**, etc. Enter the **CHORUS OF MAIDENS.**

CHORUS

I wail in the stress of my terror,
and shrill is my cry of despair.
The foemen roll forth from their camp
as a billow, and onward they bear!
Their horsemen are swift in the forefront,
the dust rises up to the sky,
A signal, though speechless, of doom,
a herald more clear than a cry!
Hoof-trampled, the land of my love
bears onward the din to mine ears.
As a torrent descending a mountain,
it thunders and echoes and nears!
The doom is unloosened and cometh!
O kings and O queens of high Heaven,
Prevail that it fall not upon us:
the sign for their onset is given—
They stream to the walls from without,
white-shielded and keen for the fray.
They storm to the citadel gates—
what god or what goddess can stay
The rush of their feet? to what shrine
shall I bow me in terror and pray?
O gods high-throned in bliss,
we must crouch at the shrines in your home!
Not here must we tarry and wail:
shield clashes on shield as they come—
And now, even now is the hour
for the robes and the chaplets of prayer!
Mine eyes feel the flash of the sword,
the clang is instinct with the spear!
Is thy hand set against us, O Ares,
in ruin and wrath to o'erwhelm
Thine own immemorial land,
O god of the golden helm?

Look down upon us, we beseech thee,
on the land that thou lovest of old,
And ye, O protecting gods,
in pity your people behold!
Yea, save us, the maidenly troop,
from the doom and despair of the slave,
For the crests of the foemen come onward,
their rush is the rush of a wave
Rolled on by the war-god's breath!
almighty one, hear us and save
From the grasp of the Argives' might!
to the ramparts of Cadmus they crowd,
And, clenched in the teeth of the steeds,
the bits clink horror aloud!
And seven high chieftains of war,
with spear and with panoply bold,
Are set, by the law of the lot,
to storm the seven gates of our hold!
Be near and befriend us, O Pallas,
the Zeus-born maiden of might!
O lord of the steed and the sea,
be thy trident uplifted to smite
In eager desire of the fray, Poseidon!
and Ares come down,
In fatherly presence revealed,
to rescue Harmonia's town!
Thine too, Aphrodite, we are!
thou art mother and queen of our race,
To thee we cry out in our need,
from thee let thy children have grace!
Ye too, to scare back the foe,
be your cry as a wolf's howl wild,
Thou, O the wolf-lord, and thou,
of she-wolf Leto the child!
Woe and alack for the sound,
for the rattle of cars to the wall,
And the creak of the grinding axles!
O Hera, to thee is our call!
Artemis, maiden beloved!
the air is distraught with the spears,
And whither doth destiny drive us,
and where is the goal of our fears?
The blast of the terrible stones
on the ridge of our wall is not stayed,
At the gates is the brazen clash
of the bucklers—Apollo to aid!
Thou too, O daughter of Zeus,
who guidest the wavering fray
To the holy decision of fate,
Athena! be with us to-day!
Come down to the sevenfold gates

and harry the foemen away!
O gods and O sisters of gods,
our bulwark and guard! we beseech
That ye give not our war-worn hold
to a rabble of alien speech!
List to the call of the maidens,
the hands held up for the right,
Be near us, protect us, and show
that the city is dear in your sight!

Have heed for her sacrifice holy,
and thought of her offerings take,
Forget not her love and her worship,
be near her and smite for her sake!

[Re-enter **ETEOCLES**.

ETEOCLES
Hark to my question, things detestable!
Is this aright and for the city's weal,
And helpful to our army thus beset,
That ye before the statues of our gods
Should fling yourselves, and scream and shriek your fears?
Immodest, uncontrolled! Be this my lot—
Never in troublous nor in peaceful days
To dwell with aught that wears a female form!
Where womankind has power, no man can house,
Where womankind feeds panic, ruin rules
Alike in house and city! Look you now—
Your flying feet, and rumour of your fears,
Have spread a soulless panic on our walls,
And they without do go from strength to strength,
And we within make breach upon ourselves!
Such fate it brings, to house with womankind.
Therefore if any shall resist my rule—
Or man, or woman, or some sexless thing—
The vote of sentence shall decide their doom,
And stones of execution, past escape,
Shall finish all. Let not a woman's voice
Be loud in council! for the things without,
A man must care; let women keep within—
Even then is mischief all too probable!
Hear ye? or speak I to unheeding ears?

CHORUS
Ah, but I shudder, child of Oedipus!
I heard the clash and clang!
The axles rolled and rumbled; woe to us
Fire-welded bridles rang!

ETEOCLES

Say—when a ship is strained and deep in brine,
Did e'er a seaman mend his chance, who left
The helm, t'invoke the image at the prow?

CHORUS
Ah, but I fled to the shrines, I called to our helpers on high,
When the stone-shower roared at the portals!
I sped to the temples aloft, and loud was my call and my cry,
Look down and deliver. Immortals!

ETEOCLES
Ay, pray amain that stone may vanquish steel!
Were not that grace of gods? ay, ay—methinks,
When cities fall, the gods go forth from them!

CHORUS
Ah, let me die, or ever I behold
The gods go forth, in conflagration dire!
The foemen's rush and raid, and all our hold
Wrapt in the burning fire!

ETEOCLES
Cry not: on Heaven, in impotent debate!
What saith the saw?—Good saving Strength, in verity,
Out of Obedience breeds the babe Prosperity.

CHORUS
'Tis true: yet stronger is the power divine,
And oft, when man's estate is overbowed
With bitter pangs, disperses from his eyne
The heavy, hanging cloud!

ETEOCLES
Let men with sacrifice and augury
Approach the gods, when comes the tug of war;
Maids must be silent and abide within.

CHORUS
By grace of the gods we hold it,
a city untamed of the spear,
And the battlement wards from the wall
the foe and his aspect of fear!
What need of displeasure herein?

ETEOCLES
Ay, pay thy vows to Heaven; I grudge them not,
But—so thou strike no fear into our men—
Have calm at heart, nor be too much afraid.

CHORUS
Alack, it is fresh in mine ears,

the clamour and crash of the fray,
And up to our holiest height
I sped on my timorous way,
Bewildered, beset by the din!

ETEOCLES
Now, if ye hear the bruit of death or wounds,
Give not yourselves o'ermuch to shriek and scream,
For Ares ravens upon human flesh.

CHORUS
Ah, but the snorting of the steeds I hear!

ETEOCLES
Then, if thou hearts, hear them not too well!

CHORUS
Hark, the earth rumbles, as they close us round!

ETEOCLES
Enough if I am here, with plans prepared.

CHORUS
Alack, the battering at the gates is loud!

ETEOCLES
Peace! stay your tongue, or else the town may hear!

CHORUS
O warders of the walls, betray them not!

ETEOCLES
Bestrew your cries! in silence face your fate.

CHORUS
Gods of our city, see me not enslaved!

ETEOCLES
On me, on all, thy cries bring slavery.

CHORUS
Zeus, strong to smite, turn upon foes thy blow!

ETEOCLES
Zeus, what a curse are women, wrought by thee!

CHORUS
Weak wretches, even as men, when cities fall.

ETEOCLES
What! clasping gods, yet voicing thy despair?

CHORUS

In the sick heart, fear machete prey of speech.

ETEOCLES

Light is the thing I ask thee—do my will!

CHORUS

Ask swiftly: swiftly shall I know my power.

ETEOCLES

Silence, weak wretch! nor put thy friends in fear.

CHORUS

I speak no more: the general fate be mine!

ETEOCLES

I take that word as wiser than the rest.
Nay, more: these images possess thy will—
Pray, in their strength, that Heaven be on our side!
Then hear my prayers withal, and then ring out
The female triumph-note, thy privilege—
Yea, utter forth the usage Hellas knows,
The cry beside the altars, sounding clear
Encouragement to friends, alarm to foes.
But I unto all gods that guard our walls,
Lords of the plain or warders of the mart
And to Isthmus' stream and Dirge's rills,
I swear, if Fortune smiles and saves our town,
That we will make our altars reek with blood
Of sheep and kine, shed forth unto the gods,
And with victorious tokens front our fannies—
Corsets and cases that once our foemen wore,
Spear-shattered now—to deck these holy homes!
Be such thy vows to Heaven—away with sighs,
Away with outcry vain and barbarous,
That shall avail not, in a general doom!
But I will back, and, with six chosen men
Myself the seventh, to confront the foe
In this great aspect of a poisèd war,
Return and plant them at the sevenfold gates,
Or e'er the prompt and clamorous battle-scouts
Haste to inflame our counsel with the need.

[Exit **ETEOCLES**.

CHORUS

I mark his words, yet, dark and deep,
My heart's alarm forbiddeth sleep!
Close-clinging cares around my soul
Enkindle fears beyond control,

Presageful of what doom may fall
From the great leaguer of the wall!
So a poor dove is faint with fear
For her weak nestlings, while anew
Glides on the snaky ravisher!
In troop and squadron, hand on hand,
They climb and throng, and hemmed we stand,
While on the warders of our town
The flinty shower comes hurtling down!

Gods born of Zeus! put forth your might
For Cadmus' city, realm, and right!
What nobler land shall e'er be yours,
If once ye give to hostile powers
The deep rich soil, and Dirce's wave,
The nursing stream, Poseidon gave
And Tethys' children? Up and save!
Cast on the ranks that hem us round
A deadly panic, make them fling
Their arms in terror on the ground,
And die in carnage! thence shall spring
High honour for our clan and king!
Come at our wailing cry, and stand
As thronèd sentries of our land!

For pity and sorrow it were
that this immemorial town
Should sink to be slave of the spear,
to dust and to ashes gone down,
By the gods of Achaean worship
and arms of Achaean might
Sacked and defiled and dishonoured,
its women the prize of the fight—
That, haled by the hair as a steed,
their mantles dishevelled and torn,
The maiden and matron alike
should pass to the wedlock of scorn!
I hear it arise from the city,
the manifold wail of despair—
Woe, woe for the doom that shall be—
as in grasp of the foeman they fare!
For a woe and a weeping it is,
if the maiden inviolate flower
Is plucked by the foe in his might,
not culled in the bridal bower!
Alas for the hate and the horror—
how say it?—less hateful by far
Is the doom to be slain by the sword,
hewn down in the carnage of war!
For wide, ah! wide is the woe
when the foeman has mounted the wall;

There is havoc and terror and flame,
and the dark smoke broods over all,
And wild is the war-god's breath,
as in frenzy of conquest he springs,
And pollutes with the blast of his lips
the glory of holiest things!

Up to the citadel rise clash and din,
The war-net closes in,
The spear is in the heart: with blood imbrued
Young mothers wail aloud,
For children at their breast who scream and die!
And boys and maidens fly,
Yet scape not the pursuer, in his greed
To thrust and grasp and feed!
Robber with robber joins, each calls his mate
Unto the feast of hate—
The banquet, lo! is spread—
seize, rend, and tear!
No need to choose or share!
And all the wealth of earth to waste is poured—
A sight by all abhorred!
The grieving housewives eye it;
heaped and blent,
Earth's boons are spoiled and spent,
And waste to nothingness; and O alas,
Young maids, forlorn ye pass—
Fresh horror at your hearts—beneath the power
Of those who crop the flower!
Ye own the ruffian ravisher for lord,
And night brings rites abhorred!
Woe, woe for you! upon your grief and pain
There comes a fouler stain.

[Enter, on one side, **THE SPY**; on the other, **ETEOCLES** and the **SIX CHAMPIONS**.

LEADER OF THE FIRST SEMI-CHORUS
Look, friends! methinks the scout, who parted hence
To spy upon the foemen, comes with news,
His feet as swift as wafting chariot-wheels.

LEADER OF THE SECOND SEMI-CHORUS
Ay, and our king, the son of Oedipus,
Comes prompt to time, to learn the spy's report—
His heart is fainter than his foot is fast!

THE SPY
Well have I scanned the foe, and well can say
Unto which chief, by lot, each gate is given.
Tydeus already with his onset-cry
Storms at the gate called Proetides; but him

The seer Amphiaraus holds at halt,
Nor wills that he should cross Ismenus' ford,
Until the sacrifices promise fair.
But Tydeus, mad with lust of blood and broil,
Like to a cockatrice at noontide hour,
Hisses out wrath and smites with scourge of tongue
The prophet-son of Oecleus—Wise thou art,
Faint against war, and holding back from death!
With such revilings loud upon his lips
He waves the triple plumes that o'er his helm
Float overshadowing, as a courser's mane;
And at his shield's rim, terror in their tone,
Clang and reverberate the brazen bells.
And this proud sign, wrought on his shield, he bears—
The vault of heaven, inlaid with blazing stars;
And, for the boss, the bright moon glows at full,
The eye of night, the first and lordliest star.
Thus with high-vaunted armour, madly bold,
He clamours by the stream-bank, wild for war,
As a steed panting grimly on his bit,
Held in and chafing for the trumpet's bray!
Whom wilt thou set against him? when the gates
Of Proetus yield, who can his rush repel?

ETEOCLES
To me, no blazon on a foeman's shield
Shall e'er present a fear! such pointed threats
Are powerless to wound; his plumes and bells,
Without a spear, are snakes without a sting.
Nay, more—that pageant of which thou tellest—
The nightly sky displayed, ablaze with stars,
Upon his shield, palters with double sense—
One headstrong fool will find its truth anon!
For, if night fall upon his eyes in death,
Yon vaunting blazon will its own truth prove,
And he is prophet of his folly's fall.
Mine shall it be, to pit against his power
The loyal son of Astacus, as guard
To hold the gateways—a right valiant soul,
Who has in heed the throne of Modesty
And loathes the speech of Pride, and evermore
Shrinks from the base, but knows no other fear.
He springs by stock from those whom Ares spared,
The men called Sown, a right son of the soil,
And Melanippus styled. Now, what his arm
To-day shall do, rests with the dice of war,
And Ares shall ordain it; but his cause
Hath the true badge of Right, to urge him on
To guard, as son, his motherland from wrong.

CHORUS

Then may the gods give fortune fair
Unto our chief, sent forth to dare
War's terrible arbitrament!
But ah! when champions wend away,
I shudder, lest, from out the fray,
Only their blood-stained wrecks be sent!

THE SPY
Nay, let him pass, and the gods' help be his!
Next, Capaneus comes on, by lot to lead
The onset at the gates Electran styled:
A giant he, more huge than Tydeus' self,
And more than human in his arrogance—
May fate forefend his threat against our walls!
God willing, or unwilling—such his vaunt—
I will lay waste this city; Pallas' self,
Zeus' warrior maid, although she swoop to earth
And plant her in my path, shall stay me not.
And, for the flashes of the levin-bolt,
He holds them harmless as the noontide rays.
Mark, too, the symbol on his shield—a man
Scornfully weaponless but torch in hand,
And the flame glows within his grasp, prepared
For ravin: lo, the legend, wrought in words,
Fire for the city bring I, flares in gold!
Against such wight, send forth—yet whom? what man
Will front that vaunting figure and not fear?

ETEOCLES
Aha, this profits also, gain on gain!
In sooth, for mortals, the tongue's utterance
Bewrays unerringly a foolish pride!
Hither stalks Capaneus, with vaunt and threat
Defying god-like powers, equipt to act,
And, mortal though he be, he strains his tongue
In folly's ecstasy, and casts aloft
High swelling words against the ears of Zeus.
Right well I trust—if justice grants the word—
That, by the might of Zeus, a bolt of flame
In more than semblance shall descend on him.
Against his vaunts, though reckless, I have set,
To make assurance sure, a warrior stern—
Strong Polyphontes, fervid for the fray;
A sturdy bulwark, he, by grace of Heaven
And favour of his champion Artemis!
Say on, who holdeth the next gate in ward?

CHORUS
Perish the wretch whose vaunt affronts our home!
On him the red bolt come,
Ere to the maiden bowers his way he cleave,

To ravage and bereave!

THE SPY
I will say on. Eteoclus is third—
To him it fell, what time the third lot sprang
O'er the inverted helmet's brazen rim,
To dash his stormers on Neistae gate.
He wheels his mares, who at their frontlets chafe
And yearn to charge upon the gates amain.
They snort the breath of pride, and, filled therewith,
Their nozzles whistle with barbaric sound.
High too and haughty is his shield's device—
An armèd man who climbs, from rung to rung,
A scaling ladder, up a hostile wall,
Afire to sack and slay; and he too cries,
(By letters, full of sound, upon the shield)
Not Ares' self shall cast me from the wall.
Look to it, send, against this man, a man
Strong to debar the slave's yoke from our town.

ETEOCLES [Pointing to **MEGAREUS**]
Send will I—even this man, with luck to aid—
By his worth sent already, not by pride
And vain pretence, is he. 'Tis Megareus,
The child of Creon, of the Earth-sprung born!
He will not shrink from guarding of the gates,
Nor fear the maddened charger's frenzied neigh,
But, if he dies, will nobly quit the score
For nurture to the land that gave him birth,
Or from the shield-side hew two warriors down
Eteoclus and the figure that he lifts—
Ay, and the city pictured, all in one,
And deck with spoils the temple of his sire!
Announce the next pair, stint not of thy tongue!

CHORUS
O thou, the warder of my home,
Grant, unto us, Fate's favouring tide,
Send on the foemen doom!
They fling forth taunts of frenzied pride,
On them may Zeus with glare of vengeance come;

THE SPY
Lo, next him stands a fourth and shouts amain,
By Pallas Onca's portal, and displays
A different challenge; 'tis Hippomedon!
Huge the device that starts up from his targe
In high relief; and, I deny it not,
I shuddered, seeing how, upon the rim,
It made a mighty circle round the shield—
No sorry craftsman he, who wrought that work

And clamped it all around the buckler's edge!
The form was Typhon: from his glowing throat
Rolled lurid smoke, spark-litten, kin of fire!
The flattened edge-work, circling round the whole,
Made strong support for coiling snakes that grew
Erect above the concave of the shield:
Loud rang the warrior's voice; inspired for war,
He raves to slay, as doth a Bacchanal,
His very glance a terror! of such wight
Beware the onset! closing on the gates,
He peals his vaunting and appalling cry!

ETEOCLES
Yet first our Pallas Onca—wardress she,
Planting her foot hard by her gate—shall stand,
The Maid against the ruffian, and repel
His force, as from her brood the mother-bird
Beats back the wintered serpent's venom'd fang
And next, by her, is Oenops' gallant son,
Hyperbius, chosen to confront this foe,
Ready to seek his fate at Fortune's shrine!

In form, in valour, and in skill of arms,
None shall gainsay him. See how wisely well
Hermes hath set the brave against the strong!
Confronted shall they stand, the shield of each
Bearing the image of opposing gods:
One holds aloft his Typhon breathing fire,
But, on the other's shield, in symbol sits
Zeus, calm and strong, and fans his bolt to flame—
Zeus, seen of all, yet seen of none to fail!
Howbeit, weak is trust reposed in Heaven—
Yet are we upon Zeus' victorious side,
The foe, with those he worsted—if in sooth
Zeus against Typhon held the upper hand,
And if Hyperbius, (as well may hap
When two such foes such diverse emblems bear)
Have Zeus upon his shield, a saving sign.

CHORUS
High faith is mine that he whose shield
Bears, against Zeus, the thing of hate.
The giant Typhon, thus revealed,
A monster loathed of gods eterne
And mortal men—this doom shall earn
A shattered skull, before the gate!

THE SPY
Heaven send it so!
A fifth assailant now
Is set against our fifth, the northern, gate,

Fronting the death-mound where Amphion lies
The child of Zeus.

This foeman vows his faith,
Upon a mystic spear-head which he deems
More holy than a godhead and more sure
To find its mark than any glance of eye,
That, will they, nill they, he will storm and sack
The hold of the Cadmeans. Such his oath—
His, the bold warrior, yet of childish years,
A bud of beauty's foremost flower, the son
Of Zeus and of the mountain maid. I mark
How the soft down is waxing on his cheek,
Thick and close-growing in its tender prime—
In name, not mood, is he a maiden's child—
Parthenopaeus; large and bright his eyes
But fierce the wrath wherewith he fronts the gate:
Yet not unheralded he takes his stand
Before the portal; on his brazen shield,
The rounded screen and shelter of his form,
I saw him show the ravening Sphinx, the fiend
That shamed our city—how it glared and moved,
Clamped on the buckler, wrought in high relief!
And in its claws did a Cadmean bear—
Nor heretofore, for any single prey,
Sped she aloft, through such a storm of darts
As now awaits her. So our foe is here—
Like, as I deem, to ply no stinted trade
In blood and broil, but traffick as is meet
In fierce exchange for his long wayfaring!

ETEOCLES
Ah, may they meet the doom they think to bring—
They and their impious vaunts—from those on high!
So should they sink, hurled down to deepest death!
This foe, at least, by thee Arcadian styled,
Is faced by one who bears no braggart sign,
But his hand sees to smite, where blows avail—
Actor, own brother to Hyperbius!
He will not let a boast without a blow
Stream through our gates and nourish our despair,
Nor give him way who on his hostile shield
Bears the brute image of the loathly Sphinx!
Blocked at the gate, she will rebuke the man
Who strives to thrust her forward, when she feels
Thick crash of blows, up to the city wall.
With Heaven's goodwill, my forecast shall be true.

CHORUS
Home to my heart the vaunting goes,
And, quick with terror, on my head

Rises my hair, at sound of those
Who wildly, impiously rave!
If gods there be, to them I plead—
Give them to darkness and the grave.

THE SPY
Fronting the sixth gate stands another foe,
Wisest of warriors, bravest among seers—
Such must I name Amphiaraus: he,
Set steadfast at the Homoloid gate,
Berates strong Tydeus with reviling words—
The man of blood, the bane of state and home,
To Argos, arch-allurer to all ill,
Evoker of the fury-fiend of hell,
Death's minister, and counsellor of wrong
Unto Adrastus in this fatal field.
Ay, and with eyes upturned and mien of scorn
He chides thy brother Polynices too
At his desert, and once and yet again
Dwells hard and meaningly upon his name
Where it saith glory yet importeth feud.
Yea, such thou art in act, and such thy grace
In sight of Heaven, and such in aftertime
Thy fame, for lips and ears of mortal men!
"He strove to sack the city of his sires
And temples of her gods, and brought on her
An alien armament of foreign foes.
The fountain of maternal blood outpoured
What power can staunch? even so, thy fatherland
Once by thine ardent malice stormed and ta'en,
Shall ne'er join force with thee." For me, I know
It doth remain to let my blood enrich
The border of this land that loves me not—
Blood of a prophet, in a foreign grave!
Now, for the battle! I foreknow my doom,
Yet it shall be with honour. So he spake,
The prophet, holding up his targe of bronze
Wrought without blazon, to the ears of men
Who stood around and heeded not his word.
For on no bruit and rumour of great deeds,
But on their doing, is his spirit set,
And in his heart he reaps a furrow rich,
Wherefrom the foison of good counsel springs.
Against him, send brave heart and hand of might,
For the god-lover is man's fiercest foe.

ETEOCLES
Out on the chance that couples mortal men,
Linking the just and impious in one!
In every issue, the one curse is this—
Companionship with men of evil heart!

A baneful harvest, let none gather it!
The field of sin is rank, and brings forth death
At whiles a righteous man who goes aboard
With reckless mates, a horde of villainy,
Dies by one death with that detested crew;
At whiles the just man, joined with citizens
Ruthless to strangers, recking nought of Heaven,
Trapped, against nature, in one net with them,
Dies by God's thrust and all-including blow.
So will this prophet die, even Oecleus' child,
Sage, just, and brave, and loyal towards Heaven,
Potent in prophecy, but mated here
With men of sin, too boastful to be wise!
Long is their road, and they return no more,
And, at their taking-off, by hand of Zeus,
The prophet too shall take the downward way.
He will not—so I deem—assail the gate—
Not as through cowardice or feeble will,
But as one knowing to what end shall be
Their struggle in the battle, if indeed
Fruit of fulfilment lie in Loxias' word.
He speaketh not, unless to speak avails!
Yet, for more surety, we will post a man,
Strong Lasthenes, as warder of the gate,
Stern to the foeman; he hath age's skill,
Mated with youthful vigour, and an eye
Forward, alert; swift too his hand, to catch
The fenceless interval 'twixt shield and spear!
Yet man's good fortune lies in hand of Heaven.

CHORUS
Unto our loyal cry, ye gods, give ear!
Save, save the city! turn away the spear,
Send on the foemen fear!
Outside the rampart fall they, rent and riven
Beneath the bolt of heaven!

THE SPY
Last, let me name yon seventh antagonist,
Thy brother's self, at the seventh portal set—
Hear with what wrath he imprecates our doom,
Vowing to mount the wall, though banished hence,
And peal aloud the wild exulting cry—
The town is ta'en—then clash his sword with thine,
Giving and taking death in close embrace,
Or, if thou 'scapest, flinging upon thee,
As robber of his honour and his home,
The doom of exile such as he has borne.
So clamours he and so invokes the gods
Who guard his race and home, to hear and heed
The curse that sounds in Polynices' name!

He bears a round shield, fresh from forge and fire,
And wrought upon it is a twofold sign—
For lo, a woman leads decorously
The figure of a warrior wrought in gold;
And thus the legend runs—I Justice am,
And I will bring the hero home again,
To hold once more his place within this town,
Once more to pace his sire's ancestral hall.
Such are the symbols, by our foemen shown—
Now make thine own decision, whom to send
Against this last opponent! I have said—
Nor canst thou in my tidings find a flaw—
Thine is it, now, to steer the course aright.

ETEOCLES
Ah me, the madman, and the curse of Heaven!
And woe for us, the lamentable line
Of Oedipus, and woe that in this house
Our father's curse must find accomplishment!
But now, a truce to tears and loud lament,
Lest they should breed a still more rueful wail!
As for this Polynices, named too well,
Soon shall we know how his device shall end—
Whether the gold-wrought symbols on his shield,
In their mad vaunting and bewildered pride,
Shall guide him as a victor to his home!
For had but Justice, maiden-child of Zeus,
Stood by his act and thought, it might have been!
Yet never, from the day he reached the light
Out of the darkness of his mother's womb,
Never in childhood, nor in youthful prime,
Nor when his chin was gathering its beard,
Hath Justice hailed or claimed him as her own.
Therefore I deem not that she standeth now
To aid him in this outrage on his home!
Misnamed, in truth, were Justice, utterly,
If to impiety she lent her hand.
Sure in this faith, I will myself go forth
And match me with him; who hath fairer claim?
Ruler, against one fain to snatch the rule,
Brother with brother matched, and foe with foe,
Will I confront the issue. To the wall!

CHORUS
O thou true heart, O child of Oedipus,
Be not, in wrath, too like the man whose name
Murmurs an evil omen! 'Tis enough
That Cadmus' clan should strive with Argos' host,
For blood there is that can atone that stain!
But—brother upon brother dealing death—
Not time itself can expiate the sin!

ETEOCLES

If man find hurt, yet clasp his honour still,
'Tis well; the dead have honour, nought beside.
Hurt, with dishonour, wins no word of praise!

CHORUS

Ah, what is thy desire?
Let not the lust and ravin of the sword
Bear thee adown the tide accursed, abhorred!
Fling off thy passion's rage, thy spirit's prompting dire!

ETEOCLES

Nay—since the god is urgent for our doom,
Let Laius' house, by Phoebus loathed and scorned,
Follow the gale of destiny, and win
Its great inheritance, the gulf of hell!

CHORUS

Ruthless thy craving is—
Craving for kindred and forbidden blood
To be outpoured—a sacrifice imbrued
With sin, a bitter fruit of murderous enmities!

ETEOCLES

Yea, my own father's fateful Curse proclaims—
A ghastly presence, and her eyes are dry—
Strike! honour is the prize, not life prolonged!

CHORUS

Ah, be not urged of her! for none shall dare
To call thee coward, in thy throned estate!
Will not the Fury in her sable pall
Pass outward from these halls, what time the gods
Welcome a votive offering from our hands?

ETEOCLES

The gods! long since they hold us in contempt,
Scornful of gifts thus offered by the lost!
Why should we fawn and flinch away from doom?

CHORUS

Now, when it stands beside thee! for its power
May, with a changing gust of milder mood,
Temper the blast that bloweth wild and rude
And frenzied, in this hour!

ETEOCLES

Ay, kindled by the curse of Oedipus—
All too prophetic, out of dreamland came
The vision, meting out our sire's estate!

LEADER OF THE CHORUS
Heed women's voices, though thou love them not!

ETEOCLES
Say aught that may avail, but stint thy words.

LEADER OF THE CHORUS
Go not thou forth to guard the seventh gate!

ETEOCLES
Words shall not blunt the edge of my resolve.

LEADER OF THE CHORUS
Yet the god loves to let the weak prevail.

ETEOCLES
That to a swordsman, is no welcome word!

LEADER OF THE CHORUS
Shall thine own brother's blood be victory's palm?

ETEOCLES
Ill which the gods have sent thou canst not shun!

[Exit **ETEOCLES**.

CHORUS
I shudder in dread of the power,
abhorred by the gods of high heaven,
The ruinous curse of the home
till roof-tree and rafter be riven!
Too true are the visions of ill,
too true the fulfilment they bring
To the curse that was spoken of old
by the frenzy and wrath of the king!
Her will is the doom of the children,
and Discord is kindled amain,
And strange is the Lord of Division,
who cleaveth the birthright in twain,—
The edged thing, born of the north,
the steel that is ruthless and keen,
Dividing in bitter division
the lot of the children of teen!
Not the wide lowland around,
the realm of their sire, shall they have,
Yet enough for the dead to inherit,
the pitiful space of a grave!

Ah, but when kin meets kin, when sire and child,
Unknowing, are defiled

By shedding common blood, and when the pit
Of death devoureth it,
Drinking the clotted stain, the gory dye—
Who, who can purify?
Who cleanse pollution, where the ancient bane
Rises and reeks again?
Whilome in olden days the sin was wrought,
And swift requital brought—
Yea on the children of the child came still
New heritage of ill!
For thrice Apollo spoke this word divine,
From Delphi's central shrine,
To Laius—Die thou childless! thus alone
Can the land's weal be won!
But vainly with his wife's desire he strove,
And gave himself to love,
Begetting Oedipus, by whom he died,
The fateful parricide!
The sacred seed-plot, his own mother's womb,
He sowed, his house's doom,
A root of blood! by frenzy lured, they came
Unto their wedded shame.
And now the waxing surge, the wave of fate,
Rolls on them, triply great—
One billow sinks, the next towers, high and dark,
Above our city's bark—
Only the narrow barrier of the wall
Totters, as soon to fall;
And, if our chieftains in the storm go down,
What chance can save the town?
Curses, inherited from long ago,
Bring heavy freight of woe:
Rich stores of merchandise o'erload the deck,
Near, nearer comes the wreck—
And all is lost, cast out upon the wave,
Floating, with none to save!

Whom did the gods, whom did the chief of men,
Whom did each citizen
In crowded concourse, in such honour hold,
As Oedipus of old,
When the grim fiend, that fed on human prey,
He took from us away?

But when, in the fulness of days,
he knew of his bridal unblest,
A twofold horror he wrought,
in the frenzied despair of his breast—
Debarred from the grace of the banquet,
the service of goblets of gold,
He flung on his children a curse

for the splendour they dared to withhold,
A curse prophetic and bitter—
The glory of wealth and of pride,
With iron, not gold, in your hands,
ye shall come, at the last, to divide!
Behold, how a shudder runs through me,
lest now, in the fulness of time,
The house-fiend awake and return,
to mete out the measure of crime!

[Enter **THE SPY**.

THE SPY
Take heart, ye daughters whom your mothers' milk
Made milky-hearted! lo, our city stands,
Saved from the yoke of servitude: the vaunts
Of overweening men are silent now,
And the State sails beneath a sky serene,
Nor in the manifold and battering waves
Hath shipped a single surge, and solid stands
The rampart, and the gates are made secure,
Each with a single champion's trusty guard.
So in the main and at six gates we hold
A victory assured; but, at the seventh,
The god that on the seventh day was born,
Royal Apollo, hath ta'en up his rest
To wreak upon the sons of Oedipus
Their grandsire's wilfulness of long ago.

LEADER OF THE CHORUS
What further woefulness besets our home?

THE SPY
The home stands safe—but ah, the princes twain—

LEADER OF THE CHORUS
Who? what of them? I am distraught with fear.

THE SPY
Hear now, and mark! the sons of Oedipus—

LEADER OF THE CHORUS
Ah, my prophetic soul! I feel their doom.

THE SPY
Have done with questions!—with their lives crushed out—

LEADER OF THE CHORUS
Lie they out yonder? the full horror speak!
Did hands meet hands more close than brotherly?
Came fate on each, and in the selfsame hour?

THE SPY

Yea, blotting out the lineage ill-starred!
Now mix your exultation and your tears,
Over a city saved, the while its lords,
Twin leaders of the fight, have parcelled out
With forged arbitrament of Scythian steel
The full division of their fatherland,
And, as their father's imprecation bade,
Shall have their due of land, a twofold grave.
So is the city saved; the earth has drunk
Blood of twin princes, by each other slain.

CHORUS

O mighty Zeus and guardian powers,
The strength and stay of Cadmus' towers!
Shall I send forth a joyous cry,
Hail to the lord of weal renewed?
Or weep the misbegotten twain,
Born to a fatal destiny?
Each numbered now among the slain,
Each dying in ill fortitude,
Each truly named, each child of feud?

O dark and all-prevailing ill,
That broods o'er Oedipus and all his line,
Numbing my heart with mortal chill!
Ah me, this song of mine,
Which, Thyad-like, I woke, now falleth still,
Or only tells of doom,
And echoes round a tomb!

Dead are they, dead! in their own blood they lie—
Ill-omened the concent that hails our victory!
The curse a father on his children spake
Hath faltered not, nor failed!
Nought, Laius! thy stubborn choice availed—
First to beget, then, in the after day
And for the city's sake,
The child to slay!
For nought can blunt nor mar
The speech oracular!
Children of teen! by disbelief ye erred—
Yet in wild weeping came fulfilment of the word!

[**ANTIGONE** and **ISMENE** approach, with a train of **MOURNERS**, bearing the bodies of **ETEOCLES** and **POLYNICES**.

Look up, look forth! the doom is plain,
Nor spake the messenger in vain!
A twofold sorrow, twofold strife—

Each brave against a brother's life!
In double doom hath sorrow come—
How shall I speak it?—on the home!

Alas, my sisters! be your sighs the gale,
The smiting of your brows the plash of oars,
Wafting the boat, to Acheron's dim shores
That passeth ever, with its darkened sail,
On its uncharted voyage and sunless way,
Far from thy beams, Apollo, god of day—
The melancholy bark
Bound for the common bourn, the harbour of the dark!
Look up, look yonder! from the home
Antigone, Ismene come,
On the last, saddest errand bound,
To chant a dirge of doleful sound,
With agony of equal pain
Above their brethren slain!
Their sister-bosoms surely swell,
Heart with rent heart according well
In grief for those who fought and fell!
Yet—ere they utter forth their woe—
We must awake the rueful strain
To vengeful powers, in realms below,
And mourn hell's triumph o'er the slain!

Alas! of all, the breast who bind,—
Yea, all the race of womankind—
O maidens, ye are most bereaved!
For you, for you the tear-drops start—
Deem that in truth, and undeceived,
Ye hear the sorrows of my heart!
[To the **DEAD**]
Children of bitterness, and sternly brave—
One, proud of heart against persuasion's voice,
One, against exile proof! ye win your choice—
Each in your fatherland, a separate grave!

Alack, on house and heritage
They brought a baneful doom, and death for wage!
One strove through tottering walls to force his way,
One claimed, in bitter arrogance, the sway,
And both alike, even now and here,
Have closed their suit, with steel for arbiter!
And lo, the Fury-fiend of Oedipus, their sire,
Hath brought his curse to consummation dire!
Each in the left side smitten, see them laid—
The children of one womb,
Slain by a mutual doom!
Alas, their fate! the combat murderous,
The horror of the house,

The curse of ancient bloodshed, now repaid!
Yea, deep and to the heart the deathblow fell,
Edged by their feud ineffable—
By the grim curse, their sire did imprecate—
Discord and deadly hate!
Hark, how the city and its towers make moan—
How the land mourns that held them for its own!
Fierce greed and fell division did they blend,
Till death made end!
They strove to part the heritage in twain,
Giving to each a gain—
Yet that which struck the balance in the strife,
The arbitrating sword,
By those who loved the twain is held abhorred—
Loathed is the god of death, who sundered each from life!
Here, by the stroke of steel, behold! they lie—
And rightly may we cry
Beside their fathers, let them here be laid—
Iron gave their doom, with iron their graves be made—
Alack, the slaying sword, alack, th' entombing spade!

Alas, a piercing shriek, a rending groan,
A cry unfeigned of sorrow felt at heart!
With shuddering of grief, with tears that start,
With wailful escort, let them hither come—
For one or other make divided moan!
No light lament of pity mixed with gladness,
But with true tears, poured from the soul of sadness,
Over the princes dead and their bereavèd home

Say we, above these brethren dead,
On citizen, on foreign foe,
Brave was their rush, and stern their blow—
Now, lowly are they laid!
Beyond all women upon earth
Woe, woe for her who gave them birth!
Unknowingly, her son she wed—
The children of that marriage-bed,
Each in the self-same womb, were bred—
Each by a brother's hand lies dead!

Yea, from one seed they sprang, and by one fate
Their heritage is desolate,
The heart's division sundered claim from claim,
And, from their feud, death came!
Now is their hate allayed,
Now is their life-stream shed,
Ensanguining the earth with crimson dye—
Lo, from one blood they sprang, and in one blood they lie!
A grievous arbiter was given the twain—
The stranger from the northern main,

The sharp, dividing sword,
Fresh from the forge and fire
The War-god treacherous gave ill award
And brought their father's curse to a fulfilment dire!
They have their portion—each his lot and doom,
Given from the gods on high!
Yea, the piled wealth of fatherland, for tomb,
Shall underneath them lie!
Alas, alas! with flowers of fame and pride
Your home ye glorified;
But, in the end, the Furies gathered round
With chants of boding sound,

Shrieking, In wild defeat and disarray,
Behold, ye pass away!
The sign of Ruin standeth at the gate,
There, where they strove with Fate—
And the ill power beheld the brothers' fall,
And triumphed over all!

ANTIGONE, ISMENE, and CHORUS [Processional Chant]
Thou wert smitten, in smiting,
Thou didst slay, and wert slain—
By the spear of each other
Ye lie on the plain,
And ruthless the deed that ye wrought was,
and ruthless the death of the twain!

Take voice, O my sorrow!
Flow tear upon tear—
Lay the slain by the slayer,
Made one on the bier!
Our soul in distraction is lost,
and we mourn o'er the prey of the spear!

Ah, woe for your ending,
Unbrotherly wrought!
And woe for the issue,
The fray that ye fought,
The doom of a mutual slaughter
whereby to the grave ye are brought!

Ah, twofold the sorrow—
The heard and the seen!
And double the tide
Of our tears and our teen,
As we stand by our brothers in death
and wail for the love that has been!

O grievous the fate
That attends upon wrong!

Stern ghost of our sire,
Thy vengeance is long!
Dark Fury of hell and of death, the hands of thy
kingdom are strong!

O dark were the sorrows
That exile hath known!
He slew, but returned not
Alive to his own!
He struck down a brother, but fell, in the moment of
triumph hewn down!

O lineage accurst,
O doom and despair!
Alas, for their quarrel,
The brothers that were!
And woe! for their pitiful end, who once were our
love and our care!

O grievous the fate
That attends upon wrong!
Stern ghost of our sire,
Thy vengeance is long!
Dark Fury of hell and of death, the hands of thy
kingdom are strong!

By proof have ye learnt it!
At once and as one,
O brothers beloved,
To death ye were done!
Ye came to the strife of the sword, and behold! ye
are both overthrown!

O grievous the tale is,
And grievous their fall,
To the house, to the land,
And to me above all!
Ah God! for the curse that hath come, the sin and
the ruin withal!

O children distraught,
Who in madness have died!
Shall ye rest with old kings
In the place of their pride?
Alas for the wrath of your sire if he findeth you laid
by his side!

[Enter a **HERALD**.

HERALD
I bear command to tell to one and all

What hath approved itself and now is law,
Ruled by the counsellors of Cadmus' town.
For this Eteocles, it is resolved
To lay him on his earth-bed, in this soil,
Not without care and kindly sepulture.
For why? he hated those who hated us,
And, with all duties blamelessly performed
Unto the sacred ritual of his sires,
He met such end as gains our city's grace,—
With auspices that do ennoble death.
Such words I have in charge to speak of him:
But of his brother Polynices, this—
Be he cast out unburied, for the dogs
To rend and tear: for he presumed to waste
The land of the Cadmeans, had not Heaven—
Some god of those who aid our fatherland—
Opposed his onset, by his brother's spear,
To whom, tho' dead, shall consecration come!
Against him stood this wretch, and brought a horde
Of foreign foemen, to beset our town.
He therefore shall receive his recompense,
Buried ignobly in the maw of kites—
No women-wailers to escort his corpse
Nor pile his tomb nor shrill his dirge anew—
Unhouselled, unattended, cast away!
So, for these brothers, doth our State ordain.

ANTIGONE
And I—to those who make such claims of rule
In Cadmus' town—I, though no other help,

[Pointing to the body of **POLYNICES**]

I, I will bury this my brother's corse
And risk your wrath and what may come of it!
It shames me not to face the State, and set
Will against power, rebellion resolute:
Deep in my heart is set my sisterhood,
My common birthright with my brothers, born
All of one womb, her children who, for woe,
Brought forth sad offspring to a sire ill-starred.
Therefore, my soul! take thou thy willing share,
In aid of him who now can will no more,
Against this outrage: be a sister true,
While yet thou livest, to a brother dead!
Him never shall the wolves with ravening maw
Rend and devour: I do forbid the thought!
I for him, I—albeit a woman weak—
In place of burial-pit, will give him rest
By this protecting handful of light dust
Which, in the lap of this poor linen robe,

I bear to hallow and bestrew his corpse
With the due covering. Let none gainsay!
Courage and craft shall arm me, this to do.

HERALD
I charge thee, not to flout the city's law!

ANTIGONE
I charge thee, use no useless heralding!

HERALD
Stern is a people newly 'scaped from death.

ANTIGONE
Whet thou their sternness! Burial he shall have.

HERALD
How? Grace of burial, to the city's foe?

ANTIGONE
God hath not judged him separate in guilt.

HERALD
True—till he put this land in jeopardy.

ANTIGONE
His rights usurped, he answered wrong with wrong.

HERALD
Nay—but for one man's sin he smote the State.

ANTIGONE
Contention doth out-talk all other gods!
Prate thou no more—I will to bury him.

HERALD
Will, an thou wilt! but I forbid the deed.

[Exit the **HERALD**.

CHORUS
Exulting Fates, who waste the line
And whelm the house of Oedipus!
Fiends, who have slain, in wrath condign,
The father and the children thus!
What now befits it that I do,
What meditate, what undergo?
Can I the funeral rite refrain,
Nor weep for Polynices slain?
But yet, with fear I shrink and thrill,
Presageful of the city's will!

Thou, O Eteocles, shalt have
Full rites, and mourners at thy grave,
But he, thy brother slain, shall he,
With none to weep or cry Alas,
To unbefriended burial pass?
Only one sister o'er his bier,
To raise the cry and pour the tear—
Who can obey such stern decree?

SEMI-CHORUS
Let those who hold our city's sway
Wreak, or forbear to wreak, their will
On those who cry, Ah, well-a-day!
Lamenting Polynices still!
We will go forth and, side by side
With her, due burial will provide!
Royal he was; to him be paid
Our grief, wherever he be laid!
The crowd may sway, and change, and still
Take its caprice for Justice' will!
But we this dead Eteocles,
As Justice wills and Right decrees,
Will bear unto his grave!
For—under those enthroned on high
And Zeus' eternal royalty—
He unto us salvation gave!
He saved us from a foreign yoke,—
A wild assault of outland folk,
A savage, alien wave!

[Exeunt.

Æschylus – A Short Biography

Æschylus is often regarded as the father of Greek tragedy, and although several others have a claim (Thespis amongst them for, as Aristophanes says, "he first decked out tragedy with magificence.") he moved play writing from the simple interaction of a single character and a chorus to one where many characters interact and thereby create more dynamic and dramatic situations.

Æschylus, was the son of Euphorion, and a scion of a Eupatrid or noble family. He was born at Eleusis 525 B.C., or, as the Greeks calculated time, in the fourth year of the 63rd Olympiad.

His first occupation was in a vineyard, and his reverence for the god of the vine inspired him to use his talents and contribute to the spectacles then newly established in honor of Dionysus. In his own words, as related to Pausanias, while still a stripling he was set to watch grapes in the country, and there fell asleep. In his slumbers Dionysus appeared to him and bade him turn his attention to the tragic art. When he awoke he made the attempt, and thus discovered his facility for dramatic composition.

It was a dream that would deliver a rich and incredible legacy through his writing talents. His earliest tragedy, composed when he was twenty-six years of age, failed to win the fabled Dionysia, and it was not until fifteen years later that he gained this victory.

Theatre was becoming a very important part of the Greek culture. The Dionysia, held annually, was the most important festival of theatre and second only to the fore-runner of the Olympic games, the Panathenia, held every four years, in appeal. It was a large festival in ancient Athens in honor of the god Dionysus, the central events of which were the theatrical performances of dramatic tragedies and, from 487 BCE, comedies. The Dionysia actually consisted of two related festivals, the Rural Dionysia and the City Dionysia, which took place in different parts of the year.

Æschylus won this revered prize in 484 BCE, 472 BCE (for The Persians), 467 BCE (for Seven Against Thebes) and 463 BCE (for The Suppliants)

Æschylus was also known for his military skills and was ready to fight in defence of Athens whenever the call was made. He and his brother, Cynegeirus, fought against Darius's invading Persian army at the Battle of Marathon in 490 BCE and, although the Greeks won against overwhelming odds, Cynegeirus died in the battle, which had a naturally had a profound effect on Æschylus.

He continued to write plays and was able to use his military experiences within many of them. The Persians were again defeated in 480BCE, this time against the invading forces of Xerese's at the Battle of Salamis. This naval battle holds a prominent place in "The Persians", his oldest surviving play, which was performed in 472 BCE and won first prize at the Dionysia. In fact, by 473 BCE, after the death of his chief rival, Phrynichus, Æschylus was winning first prize in nearly every competition at the Dionysia.

Æschylus was also an adherent of the Eleusinian Mysteries, a mystical, secretive cult dedicated to the Earth-mother goddess Demeter, which was based in his hometown of Eleusis.

He made several visits to the important Greek city of Syracuse in Sicily at the invitation of the tyrant Hieron, and it is thought that he also travelled extensively in the region of Thrace.

His writing continued to be the envy of others. With the series of plays of which Seven Against Thebes was a part, his supremacy was undisputed. He was the "father of tragedy"

Æschylus made many changes to dramatic form. The importance of the chorus was demoted and a second added to give prominence to the dialogue and making that interchange the leading feature of the play. He removed all deeds of bloodshed from the public view, and in their place provided various spectacular elements, improving the costumes, making the masks more expressive and convenient, and probably adopting the cothurnus to increase the stature of the performers. Finally, he established the custom of contending for the prize with trilogies; an inter-connecting set of three independent dramas.

The closing years of the life of Æschylus were mainly spent in Sicily, which he had first visited soon after his defeat at the Dionysia by Sophocles. Whilst in Syracuse his Persæ was performed several times at the specific request of the king, and whilst here he brought out his Women of Etna, celebrating the foundation of that city by Hiero and prophesying happiness for its inhabitants.

Æschylus returned to Athens to produce his Orestean trilogy, probably the finest of his works, although the Eumenides, the last of the three plays, revealed so openly his aristocratic tendencies that he became extremely unpopular, and returned to Sicily.

The farewell lines in which Æschylus seems to bid goodbye to his beloved Athens, which at his time of life he would hardly have hoped to see again, occur in the Eumenides. They are a long reverent salutation of Athens, her gods, her laws and customs, full of exhortations to trusted old-established institutions, and the call to preserve them from the arbitrary caprice of innovators, while invoking all blessings on the inhabitants.

Rejoice, rejoice ye in abounding wealth,
Rejoice, ye citizens,
Dwelling near Zeus himself,
Loved of the virgin goddess whom ye love,
In due time wise of heart,
You, 'neath the wings of Pallas ever staying,
The Father honoreth.

Rejoice, rejoice once more, ye inhabitants!
I say it yet again,
Ye gods and mortals too,
Who dwell in Pallas' city. Should ye treat
With reverence us who dwell
As sojourners among you, ye shall find
No cause to blame your lot.
Accused of Impiety

According to Ælian, Clemens Alexandrinus and others, Æschylus was accused of impiety before the court of Areopagus, and this there seems no reason to doubt, notwithstanding the honors paid to him after death, for the Athenians were the most fickle of communities. Among other charges it was alleged that in one of his plays he had revealed the Eleusinian mysteries, and this was probably in the Eumenides, which is full of references to religious subjects. It is even said that his life was threatened while on the stage, and that he only saved himself by taking refuge at the altar of Dionysus.

If, in his political opinions he inclined to the aristocratic party, to which he belonged by birth, he was essentially patriotic, constantly warning the people to make a moderate use of their freedom, to avoid all blustering and excess, and especially to preserve the venerable court of the Areopagus, from which the democratic party had tried to wrest its power. Of this we have sufficient evidence in his verse, which, as Aristophanes says, "taught only the good and the true."

He returned to Sicily for the last time in 458 BCE and it was there that he died, while visiting the city of Gela in 456 or 455 BCE.

His death was embellished into fable telling that an eagle, mistaking his bald head for a stone, dropped a tortoise upon it to break the shell, an obvious fabrication, and, it would seem, entirely unnecessary to account for the natural death of an exile nearly seventy years of age.

Interestingly, the inscription on Æschylus' gravestone makes no mention of his theatrical renown, commemorating only his military achievements.

This tomb the dust of Æschylus doth hide,
Euphorion's son and fruitful Gela's pride;
How tried his valor Marathon may tell,
And long-haired Medes, who knew it all too well.

In the tone of his works we recognize the high-minded Athenian whose sword had drunk at Marathon and Salamis the blood of long-haired Medes. His plays abound in military terms, and while breathing the utmost contempt for barbarian prowess, he often introduces on the stage the grotesque monsters whose images he had seen among the spoils of Persian camps. Even his diction is of the military type, his sonorous words striking on the ear like trumpet-sounds. Yet he held his own dramas in light esteem, declaring that they were but crumbs from the great banquet of Homer.

"Not only," says one of his critics, "had he fought at Marathon and Salamis against those Persians whose rout he celebrated with patriotic pride, but he had been trained in the Eleusinian mysteries, and was a passionate upholder of the institution most intimately associated with the political traditions of the past—the Areopagus. He had been born in the generation after Solon, to whose maxims he fondly clung; he belonged to that anti-democratic party which favored the Spartan alliance, and it was the Dorian development of Hellenic life and the philosophical system based on it with which his religious and moral convictions were imbued. Thus, even upon the generations which succeeded him the chivalrous spirit and diction of his poetry, and the unapproached sublimity of his dramatic imagination, fell, as it falls upon later posterity, like the note of a mightier age."

Such is the wonderful power of art in its highest forms, that tragedy, and never treated with the same effect by their countless imitators, has ever been held the gravest, most moral and most profitable of all forms of poetry.

"Why is it," asks a classical scholar, "that we thrill with horror when the death-cry of Agamemnon announces the wreaking of his doom? It is because in this and all other instances of the art of the Greek drama, while winged by the individual power of genius, is at the same time true to its purposes as an art, and in perfect harmony with Nature, who does not readily yield her secrets or teach her laws to all."

Æschylus was the only man of his age, or indeed of any age, who can compare with the great master of the modern drama in sublimity of conception and grandeur of poetic imagery. As to the esteem in which he was held by his contemporaries and his immediate posterity there is sufficient evidence, and first in the Frogs of Aristophanes, who there describes his temper as proud, stern and impatient; his sentiments as pure, noble and warlike; his genius inventive, magnificent and towering; his style lofty, bold and impetuous, full of gorgeous imagery and ponderous expressions, while in the dramatic arrangement of his pieces there remained much of ancient simplicity and somewhat of uncouth rudeness. Dionysius of Halicarnassus lauds the splendor of his talents, the propriety of his characters, the originality of his ideas and the force, variety and beauty of his language. Longinus speaks of the bold magnificence of his imagery, though condemning some of his conceptions as rude and turgid and his expressions as sometimes overstrained. Quintilian ascribes to him dignity of sentiment, sublimity of ideas and loftiness in style, yet often overcharged in diction and irregular in composition. Such, as seen through the eyes of antiquity, was the Shakespeare of the Greeks.

Æschylus – A Concise Bibliography

The Surviving Plays

The Persians
The Suppliants
Seven Against Thebes

Agamemnon (Part I of "The Oresteia)
The Libation Bearers" (Part II of "The Oresteia)
The Eumenides (Part III of The Oresteia)
Prometheus Bound

The Lost Plays

Over seventy plays are no longer with us. However from fragments that do remain as well as accounts both then and in later times a catalogue can be assembled and with it the basic plot of several of them.

Myrmidons
This play was based on books 9 and 16 in Homer's Iliad. Achilles sits in silent indignation over his humiliation at Agamemnon's hands for most of the play. Envoys from the Greek army attempt to reconcile him to Agamemnon, but he yields only to his friend Patroclus, who then battles the Trojans in Achilles' armour. The bravery and death of Patroclus are reported in a messenger's speech, which is followed by mourning.

Nereids
This play was based on books 18, 19, and 22 of the Iliad; it follows the Daughters of Nereus, the sea god, who lament Patroclus' death. In the play, a messenger tells how Achilles, perhaps reconciled to Agamemnon and the Greeks, slew Hector.

Phrygians, or Hector's Ransom
In this play, Achilles sits in silent mourning over Patroclus, after a brief discussion with Hermes. Hermes then brings in King Priam of Troy, who wins over Achilles and ransoms his son's body in a spectacular coup de théâtre. A scale is brought on stage and Hector's body is placed in one scale and gold in the other. The dynamic dancing of the chorus of Trojans when they enter with Priam is reported by Aristophanes.

Niobe
The children of Niobe, the heroine, have been slain by Apollo and Artemis because Niobe had gloated that she had more children than their mother, Leto. Niobe sits in silent mourning on stage during most of the play. In the Republic, Plato quotes the line "God plants a fault in mortals when he wills to destroy a house utterly."

Listed below are the other titles ascribed to Æschylus:

Alcmene
Amymone
The Archer-Women
The Argivian Women
The Argo, also titled The Rowers
Atalanta
Athamas
Attendants of the Bridal Chamber
Award of the Arms
The Bacchae
The Bassarae
The Bone-Gatherers

The Cabeiroi
Callisto
The Carians, also titled Europa
Cercyon
Children of Hercules
Circe
The Cretan Women
Cycnus
The Danaids
Daughters of Helios
Daughters of Phorcys
The Descendants
The Edonians
The Egyptians
The Escorts
Glaucus of Pontus
Glaucus of Potniae
Hypsipyle
Iphigenia
Ixion
Laius
The Lemnian Women
The Lion
Lycurgus
Memnon
The Men of Eleusis
The Messengers
The Myrmidons
The Mysians
Nemea
The Net-Draggers
The Nurses of Dionysus
Orethyia
Palamedes
Penelope
Pentheus
Perrhaibides
Philoctetes
Phineus
The Phrygian Women
Polydectes
The Priestesses
Prometheus the Fire-Bearer
Prometheus the Fire-Kindler
Prometheus Unbound
Proteus
Semele, also titled The Water-Bearers
Sisyphus the Runaway
Sisyphus the Stone-Roller
The Spectators, also titled Athletes of the Isthmian Games
The Sphinx

The Spirit-Raisers
Telephus
The Thracian Women
Weighing of Souls
Women of Aetna (two versions)
Women of Salamis
Xantriae
The Youths

www.ingramcontent.com/pod-product-compliance
Lightning Source LLC
Chambersburg PA
CBHW060103050426
42448CB00011B/2605